david bowie

glass idol

text: david currie

design: gina coyle & david currie

Omnibus Press
London/New York/Sydney/Cologne

David Bowie: Glass Idol
Written by David Currie
Design by Gina Coyle and David Currie
Photo-research by David Currie
Text Editor: Chris Charlesworth

© Copyright 1987 Omnibus Press/David Currie
(A Division of Book Sales Limited)

ISBN 0.7119.1182.7
Order No. OP 44411

Exclusive distributors:
Book Sales Limited
8/9 Frith Street, London W1V 5TZ, UK.

Music Sales Corporation
24 East 22nd Street, New York,
NY 10010, USA.

Music Sales Pty. Limited
GPO Box 3304, Sydney,
NSW 2001, Australia.

To the Music Trade only:
Music Sales Limited
8/9 Frith Street, London W1V 5TZ, UK.

Typeset by Capital Setters

Printed in England
by Eyre & Spottiswoode Ltd,
London and Margate.

Photograph credits:

David Currie: *Page 1, 5, 16 (Bottom Left), 20,
25 (Bottom), 26/27, 28, 36 (Top), 41, 43
(Bottom), 51 (Inset), 52 (Left), 54, 59, 61, 62
(Top Right and Bottom Right), 63 (Top and
Bottom Left), 64, 68, 70/71, 83 (Right), Back
Cover (Top).*
Robin Prichard: *Page 18, 19, 30/31, 32 (Top
Right), 37, 49, 50 (Right), 51, 53 (Right), 55,
58 (Inset), 62 (Top Left), 63 (Top and Bottom
Right), 65, 69, 77, 81 (Bottom), 82, 85, 86/87,
88, 92 – 95, Back Cover (Bottom).*
Ger Peeters: *Page 4, 24, 25 (Top), 32 (Left and
Bottom Right), 35, 36 (Bottom), 38, 39, 42, 43
(Top), 48, 50 (Left and Bottom), 52/53
(Middle), 55 (Inset), 58, 60, 67, 74, 75, 76, 80,
81 (Top, 83 (Left).*
Marco Rossi: *7, 8, 9, 12, 57 (Middle), 90.*
Aad Rijnsbergen: *11, 16 (Bottom Right), 57
(Middle Right and Bottom.)*
Dave Foster: *33, 44.*
C. Spruyt: *16 (Top), 23 (Top), 66, 91 (Bottom).*
Alan Casse: *40, 64 (Inset), 72, 73.*
EMI Records: *13.*
Nico Kruithof: *23 (Bottom), 57 (Top).*
Rob Verhorst: *17.*
Nicky Young: *91 (Top).*
Tim Bauer: *96.*
The author expresses his thanks to all
photographers·

CONTENTS

INTRODUCTION

In 1987, David Bowie embarked on the most ambitious world tour of his entire career. A career already illustrious and dotted with a staggering amount of untouchable triumphs.

His vision, to return to a world of rock theatre at a time in his life when past mistakes were rectified – to re-establish his stance as a performance-artist – was boldly conceptualised with the Glass Spider tour.

It is estimated that by the time the tour finished, Bowie and his band had played to a total of over three million people, beating his previous record set by the 1983 Serious Moonlight tour.

This book offers a durable record of the European leg of the tour, drawing from just a small portion of the three million that attended the shows. The emotions, expectations and delights of the fans all play a major role in the theme of the writing.

It is they that have made David Bowie a Glass Idol – a delicate, fragile individual, listened to intently, viewed incessantly. What they conceive and what he offers form the basis of stardom and the trappings therein.

David Bowie is one rare example of such an idol. One that has reached maturity derived from understanding and, at times, sheer calculation. It is he to whom they flock and it is they to whom he sings.

David Currie, Summer 1987

PART ONE

FACTS AND SECRETS

The poster announcing a London concert had been up seconds only before a fan ripped it down, folded its glue-sodden body to pocket-size and hid it away. Some prize.

The time it would take for a rock star to give a press conference and maybe sing a couple of songs would be enough for the glue to harden, leaving a papier mâché dumpling in the fan's jacket. But this wasn't about high stakes commodity, or even self-preening elitism – this was about rock 'n' roll.

So the stolen poster was all right. Expected. Just as expected as those crowds of fans that always gather around places they really shouldn't, at times some thankless person had gone to great pains to conceal. Position a rock star on any remote corner of the globe and the fans will be **expected** to be there. Some may curse them, others praise them. But all will expect them.

To announce his 1987 European tour, David Bowie chose to discard star trappings and return to basics. Here he was 40-years old, self-invented man, good-and-I-know it – another comfortable position for another collection of songs.

With a total of nine press conferences, he played live and fielded questions from journalists in Toronto, New York, London, Paris, Rome, Amsterdam,

▲ **The Wembley announcement**

Madrid, Munich and Stockholm. During the conferences he also, and this is where the expected one's plans bore fruit, allowed fans to join the select throng.

"Whose idea was it to let you lot in?" cried Bowie in Amsterdam in his best chummy voice, *"Mine, o'course!"*

Thus, past sins forgiven, David Bowie once again seduced his audience back into his way of thinking. No more the iceman cometh but now wielding an open invitation for everyone to join him for a drink while he tells you whose concerts you should be seeing in the summer.

Repayment? Insecurity? Sincerity? Good business sense? Remembering that David's own past publicity has informed us that 'One man in his time plays many parts', the smart money would be spread equally over all four.

Bowie's press conferences marked an utter dispensing of the tight-lipped slickness of 1983. He handled them like a well-trained diplomat, stymieing awkward questions and offering only peripheral answers to direct ones. He revealed to what extent he had come to terms with not only his own mortality but also the worth of past glories. He sniggered affectionately at Ziggy (*"Ziggy's back in an infirmary back in 1973"*), delighted in his experimental phase and agreed that the mammoth 1983 Serious Moonlight tour was purely an exercise to make money and remind people of the quality of the songs he'd written.

◀ **Fans in high spirits after the Player's press conference**

"No, I'm not worried about competition this
▼ year. Prince is only this high!"

"What's that? Prince's lawyer is on the phone? Tell him I'm in Berlin." ▶

Proving that in face-to-face confrontations most journalists have little of relevance to ask, the questions ranged from the painfully obvious to the downright ridiculous. (*"Who did you write 'God Only Knows' for?"*)

Perhaps the most eloquent statement about the performer's confidence in his new material was the live rendition of songs. After all, playing live in a tiny theatre to a group of chisel-faced hacks could have spelt critical death.

But Bowie chuckled his way throughout each and every one of the conferences — winning more by intimidation of presence rather than anything else.

This strange and unpredictable way of announcing the tour grew more curious still as only scattered dates were offered at each conference. Even as the tour opened, a full itinerary had yet to be established. Members of the band only received their first communication regarding departure times and future travelling arrangements the night before the first show.

Bowie's 1987 touring plans were not that hastily organised, however, despite the surface appearance. Tentative bookings for venues and a red alert for those involved went out at the beginning of 1986. Isolar, his management company in New York, leapt into action, making enquiries, assembling personnel, routinely checking the possible trajectory of the touring party. Although embryonic, the sudden activity marked a definite nod from Bowie's tousled head.

Isolar worried over physical details while Bowie himself used the 12 months of 1986 to decide the nature and tone of his first tour in four years.

Serious Moonlight, due to its sheer scale and ultimate triumph, would be a tough act to follow. Bowie's global stature as a performer was relatively small compared to multi-million selling others before 1983, but the 'Let's Dance' explosion fully established him as a com-

mercially powerful artiste.

But Bowie knew that you can't run the same mile twice. Repetition would mean mud-shots, anything less would mean derision. *"I needed time to decide for myself which audience I would continue to write for,"* said Bowie. *"Eventually I decided to be true to myself and write music I enjoyed."*

The result was the album 'Never Let Me Down', admittedly written by direct influence of Iggy Pop — a small-band sound, raw and tight — lyrically direct with touches of the Bowie ambiguity that so typified his music of 1970's. *"It's a progression from 'Scary Monsters' rather than my last two albums,"* said Bowie. *"It's almost like there's no break between the*

Signing autographs during rehearsals in Rotterdam ▶

two.'' The album took just three months to write and record – Bowie, in fact, hitting a new vein of inspiration and over-writing by at least eight songs. A more optimistic trend than the harrowing struggle of 'Tonight' (1984). Although 'Never Let Me Down' gained few accolades from the music press, NME called it *"A pieced together product that tries to hit all the correct mass response buttons"* while Melody Maker considered it *"Wilfully lacking grandeur"*.

The album thundered into the charts and just as boldly thundered out again. Success in moderation was not a familiar occurrence around the Bowie camp in the high-profile eighties – was Bowie possibly making himself *too* accessible?

The two main musicians on the album were faithful *Carlos Alomar* and a fresh discovery by Bowie – a Turkish, multi-talented instrumentalist, *Erdal Kizilcay*, whom Bowie spotted displaying his varied skills in clubs in Switzerland. During interviews, Bowie regularly enthused about the unknown in much the same way as he had about *Stevie Ray-Vaughn,* the Texan guitarist who overstepped the mark and fell from favour just before the 1983 tour.

Bowie, it seems, would never fail to promote a particular member of his band – just so long as it was on his terms. This apparent generosity would explain the passionate devotion offered by appreciative musicians and the inherent fear felt by those less so.

The biggest surprise of all was the addition of one-time guitar hero *Peter Frampton* to the band.

Bowie had maintained sporadic contact with Frampton since their Bromley school days, though he had never worked with the guitarist before.

"When we were recording the album," Frampton recalled, *"it was constantly, 'Do you remember so and so from school?' But that quickly wore off and it was down to business."*

From Frampton's band came Welshman *Richard Cottle* on keyboards, leaving Carlos to assemble the final band members who would constitute Bowie's '87 tour group.

Carmine Rojas returned from the '83 band – he and Carlos had developed a strong brother-like association, something which pleased Bowie and increased camaraderie.

Both New Yorker Puerto Ricans, Alomar and Rojas had worked together on unrelated projects in New York, together

During the promotional tour

with drummer *Alan Childs* (or 'Lad', 'Young' – depending on Bowie's moods at individual shows), who joined the '87 band through that connection. Receiving The Phone Call around June 1986, the band was given no detailed brief as to the nature of the tour, just the clipped instruction: 'Be ready for next year.'

March 1987, and the circus began with tickets for stadium-sized shows going on sale across Europe.

Britain adopted a credit card hot-line system through which the majority of tickets for Bowie's UK dates were swiftly grabbed up. *"We sold 70 per cent of tickets that way,"* said a leading promoter. *"Some people must have had a shock when they saw their statements!"* Across Europe tickets sold out at lightning speed, with people queuing nights on end for their prized piece of paper.

In Amsterdam riots ensued, resulting in people being pushed through the ticket office windows. Further riots and fighting became a frequent occurrence among many winding queues of bedraggled, tired and often inebriated would-be concert goers.

In a rock summer touted as being the most exciting ever, with many monster bands going out, the scramble for Bowie tickets left little doubt that he was the hottest of them all.

**Two scenes from the banned 'Day In, Day Out' video that focused on the plight of the homeless in society.
The video was ruthlessly cut and eventually shown, in nonsensical form on British television.** ▶

REHEARSALS AND HUNTED

PART TWO

Announcements and general introductions over, tour rumours, now confirmed, changed quickly into spurious gossip as to the format of the show and finger-to-the-nose asides regarding Bowie's promised theatrics.

Oblivious, or perhaps highly amused by all this, Bowie and entourage began solid, 12-hour-a-day rehearsals in New York – a maddened dash to bring together all elements of the show – band, dancers, lights, stage moves, before the premiere show in Holland on May 30.

These rehearsals, studious and applied, lasted three weeks with the singular centre of the cyclone alternating his attention between the musical and physical aspects of the ambitious show.

Band leader *Carlos Alomar* assumed responsibility, as he had for the past 14 years, to rehearse the band and give expression to the music in his typically intuitive way that would render a Bowie tour without him an unthinkable prospect.

"I'm responsible for 99½ per cent of the music," Carlos commented. *"David would bring me an initial list of around 30 songs he'd want to perform. I would listen to the original songs and then re-arrange the older material to sound similar in style to the newer ones – ultimately giving one continuous musical frame."*

Bowie's selection of material for the Glass Spider tour drew mainly from his 1980's product, with only one or two isolated pickings from his pre-Scary Monsters catalogue.

Flatly denied as a 'golden oldies' tour, à la Serious Moonlight, Bowie's intentions were not as fundamentally commercially based as in 1983, giving him a much wider scope for presentation. As Alomar observed: *"This is the most rock 'n' roll orientated tour David has ever done. The songs were all chosen to be loud and hard. And yet, it's theatre. We've got the biggest set in rock history and we're undertaking the most physically dangerous tour I've*

◀ **Fans camp out at 'de Kuip' for the premiere**

Faithful Carlos Alomar – Bowie's bandleader for 15 years. ▼

ever known." (Insurance policies on each tour member grew enormous and myriad.) *"No doubt about it, we're taking bold chances – but then, everything with David is a test."*

With the musical side securely in Alomar's capable hands, Bowie focused his attention on the stage gimmickry and choreography, taking an active role in almost every aspect of the show's formation – from dance routines to scaffolding problems.

One such problem, Bowie was informed by the construction crew, would take three months to solve – and, as the story goes, one repeated with gusto by tour personnel – Bowie arrived at a workable solution in just half an hour.

"David can do anyone's job," said *Toni Basil,* who was brought in when plans were in their infancy to assist Mr Jack-of-all-trades to choreograph the six dancers, all close associates of Ms Basil and hand-picked for the show by herself and David. One, *Viktor Manoei,* was an unknown New York street dancer until Bowie saw videos of him and picked him instantly.

Despite the constant pressure to create, quickly, a balanced fusion between dance and music, rehearsals were light-hearted affairs – frequently punctuated with comical observations and rambunctious jokes. *"With the stress and tensions of the day,"* said Bowie, *"vulgarity of any nature makes the biggest break-through in the comedy stakes!"*

This absence of the superstar's heavy hand is an unaffected Bowie trait that would wreck any preconceptions of the-man-as-an-ego-monster and go some way

▲ **L to R: Constance Marie, Stephen Nichols, Viktor Manoei and Spazz Attack.**

▲ **Carlos waves goodbye . . . .**

▲ **Frampton signs autographs . . . .**

◀

Three members of the band – all taken at the Rotterdam Hilton

to explain musicians' devotion to giving him their very best.

David Bowie is no stranger to rock 'n' roll tours and is fully aware of how a six-month worldwide trek could quickly develop into a torturous endurance test unless morale is high.

"Touring with David is just like a fun outing," chortled bassist Carmine Rojas. *"We're all way beyond the stupidity of rock 'n' roll. People that behave like superstars are just insecure about themselves. The way you see us onstage is the way we are in reality."*

Monday, May 18, exactly four years after the première of the Moonlight tour in Brussels, the tour company moved to Rotterdam to commence battle-field condition rehearsals at the Ahoy Sports-palace, a venue Bowie had previously played in 1978. The 60-foot vacuum-cleaner legged spider was erected, looming nonchalantly over the smooth-paced proceedings below. Scrambling bodies, flashing vari-lites and fragmented songs.

The final countdown had begun and the future success of the tour would depend largely on the successful culmination of all those ideas born in eagerness weeks before.

Bowie was noticeably calm and seemingly unshakeably confident both on and off stage. Staying at the Rotterdam Hilton, together with all tour personnel, for such a lengthy period, Bowie was easy prey for the multitude of fervent Dutch fans who quickly detected his presence.

"I decided to start the tour in Holland because I wanted to begin in a place with an audience that had an affinity with my work," Bowie had said earlier in the year. *"And it seemed that Holland had been with me for such a long time that it would be nice to start there."*

Indeed, Dutch Bowie fans are among his most avid worldwide, deeply appreciative and with an inexhaustible devotion to the man. Swiftly, and with the precision of a game hunter, they posted sentries at the

◀ **and Carmine advertises.**

◀ **Photographed during the first Glass Spider show**

Ahoy – taping rehearsals and snatching meetings and autographs from Bowie as he came and went, morning or evening.

Weeks before the first show, and well ahead of any unscrupulous press, the fans knew the songs to be played (although two songs rehearsed, 'Because You're Young' and 'Scream Like A Baby' – both from the 'Scary Monsters' album – were eventually dropped from the final selection), had glimpsed the Glass Spider and gained access to the star himself.

Bowie greeted their discoveries with congenial charm. This was, after all, to be a fan's tour – a return to form for those that remembered more callow days when to be a Bowie fan meant, more often than not, you had to defend his name against the mainstream.

Meanwhile, the lumbering administration machine shifted gears, leaving previously unresolved problems in the dust. Who's getting press tickets? Photo passes? Is the ink dry on the programmes? Will the cable that lowers the chair at the start of the show yield a jerk-free descent? At what hour will the lights give maximum impact? Check this, check that, then check it all again. The total number of figures, statistics and mundane necessities needed to create a spectacle as gargantuan as this would fill any stadium. Imagine simply, the organisation required to ensure 43 trucks carrying just one spider set (of three) reach their destinations intact and on time.

600,000 watts worth of light power would be rendered useless if someone had forgotten to carry spare fuses.

150 personnel, taking care of anything you'd care to mention, (though not including the local set erectors) need to be fed, watered, transported and well kept. The days of a Bowie tour neatly condensed into a couple of Greyhound coaches were long gone. Big business breeds big organisation and even bigger headaches. Welcome to 1987.

The linchpin in the entire mobile con-

struction was also kept busy. Ironing out voice problems to discover the most workable pitch level to apply to individual songs, exercising religiously to increase stamina – a vital element to ensure the high endurance rate needed to last two hours a night of very physical theatre. Appearance was closely checked and improved. This was Bowie's first middle-aged step into the spotlight. By his own dedication, there would be no 'crock 'n' roll' headlines.

On May 22, Bowie gave a live interview to Rotterdam's Radio Rijnmond, transmitted worldwide via satellite. It was held at a public café which, predictably, was soon crammed full of onlookers and saucer-eyed devotees. Accessibility by

▲ **More Dutch autographs**

sight seemed the subtitle for this tour.

During the interview, a local artist worked feverishly to complete a large oil painting of David in the hope that the star might pause to look at the work after the questions had finished and maybe even add his signature to it.

The painting was completed in under an hour and was hung, still wet, on a wall facing Bowie. Due to the ever-swelling crowds, Bowie made his exit from the back of the café, and the painting never fell before his mis-matched eyes. The café developed into a popular meeting place for fans attending the Rotterdam shows soon after – as the local Dutch fans regaled visiting concert-goers from England, France and America with many tales of Bowie's prolonged stay in the city. *"Oh yeah,"* was the casual comment, *"David was here just the other day. He looks just like his pictures, you know."*

Finally, the whole stage was transported from the Ahoy to the Feyenoord Stadium, colloquially referred to as 'de Kuip', on May 25 and rehearsals continued steadfastly, sometimes with and sometimes without Bowie.

There now remained only days before the premiere of the Glass Spider tour and any pre-show nerves from Bowie and the band were well hidden, tempered with a cool exterior belying the natural antici-

◄ **A hug for Melissa Hurley during 'Bang, Bang.'**

24

▼ **Visiting fans soon found the 'Bowie Cafe'.**

pation felt by those poised on the very top of a pending helter skelter ride.

"*We're totally in control of our own environment,*" Carlos said to me on the morning before the first show, his constant beaming smile lending weight to his words.

"*We want this show to be Baaad and we're taking a lot of chances to impress the audience.*

"*David has changed so much since I first worked with him. But he's not getting older, he's getting better. In 1974 he was a wimp who didn't like confrontations and let people walk all over him. Now he's a mad ass-kicker, in control of every aspect of his life. He'd scream at you now if the need arose. There's absolutely no question of him taking any steps backward.*"

Forward, then.

Glass
idol

WEB-WORK

PART THREE

As expected, the city of Rotterdam held court to a constant stream of fans, reporters and the just plain curious leading up to and during the first Glass Spider shows which were on the Saturday and Sunday of May 30 and 31.

By car, train, tram and by foot they congregated early at the Kuip, camping in large clusters around the entrance gates, preparing for the free-for-all sprint to the front of the stage. Unofficial merchandise was sold openly outside the venue, ink-

blotted t-shirts, scarfs and posters that were so hastily produced most items had many of the tour dates wrongly specified. Ticket touts were out in force – most of them English, with seemingly two separate groups from London and the North. They paraded their tickets like prostitutes bartering and selling but predominantly deceiving and conning any unsuspecting patron. One individual even tried to sell an identity card, issued to stadium employees who were giving out freebie magazines, as a back-stage pass! It shall go unrecorded as to whether or not he was successful.

At 5.00pm the floodgates opened, creating a back-thumping crush – in went the hot bodies, cameras and cassette recorders and even video cameras. The intricate methods used by fans to smuggle

in such equipment are often ingenious and well planned. It would be remiss of me to offer examples and thus spoil the rules of the game.

Inside the stadium, the audience, those fleet-footed enough, sat and sweltered in front of the stage for up to five hours. They discussed the Glass Spider, unveiled to the public for the first time, donned their official t-shirts, delegated the buying of food and drink and began a constant avoidance of people – walking backwards, sideways, forward. If a mega-tour demands a high endurance factor from its practitioners, then it also sets a high price in discomfort, tedium and stamina for the audience.

It would not take a great deal of inside information for any distracted observer to realise the changes in David Bowie over the last 15 years. Nowadays, in direct contrast to a time when his audience were highly select and often with an attitude-problem towards non-Bowie fans, he pulls in new generations of more fickle followers – content to follow the summer-stadium packs. This week it's Bowie, the high cheek-boned English eccentric – next week, it could be *Genesis* or *Prince* or *U2*.

Glass Spider was the first all stadium tour for Bowie – no messing around with anything less than 60,000 capacity – he had a reputation to live up to, and, due to

▲ **The unofficial traders**

28

Bowie's spectacular show debut ▶

personal investment in the tour running into millions, a lot of finance to consider.

It's of some credit to the performer that, despite the absence of intimacy given by such shows, his choice for presentation harkened back to the experimental and chance-taking tours of the 70's. *"Our biggest concern is that the cameras catch all the action on stage,"* said Alomar. *"This tour has more substance than any other and*

we want people to enjoy it. In some respects, it's unfortunate that these venues are the only feasible way of staging the show, but we're not going to let that way of thinking stop us."

▼ **Constance and Spazz in a subdued moment**

▲ **Revived from 1974 – the old telephone trick**

"It's chicken and feathers! It's like kissing a blow-torch! It's rock 'n' roll!!"

It's the wrong side of 9.00pm when the première of the Glass Spider show begins.

People, cramped and weary now after two hours standing as one huddled mass, pushed in waves from every direction, avoiding the sporadic fights and trying hard to take in enough air not to faint. This is where the grim determination to enjoy a concert comes into play.

As Alomar rushes forward on-stage, the clear signal to commence battle-stations, the crowd also surges. *WE WANT TO SEE BOWIE.* Carlos throttles his guitar, filling the stadium with pure energy, the crowds scream in unison – a voice interrupts the melée: *"SHUT UP!"*

60,000 people and the 'hardest working Puerto Rican in rock comply. But only for an instant. Carlos returns to his solo, the disembodied voice shouts again, louder, Carlos retaliates only to be told, for a third and final time, to stop.

During this discourse, from the sides of the spider, the dancers are lowered by ropes. They look ridiculous and sinister in their red Voodoo masks. Very theatrical but still no Bowie.

A chant-like version of 'Up The Hill Backwards' follows, pleasing many with the return to familiar territory but, purposely, alienating all with the rendition.

At last, as the murmured introduction to 'Glass Spider' strikes up, Bowie's voice, still heard from behind the scenes, resounds over the sound system.

A study of delight – Just part of the three million ▲

Radio mikes gave Bowie more stage freedom

Then, he is visible. He doesn't saunter on-stage from the wings, or even run on swiftly. Slowly, picked out by a single white spotlight, Bowie is lowered from the belly of the spider construct, seated kingly in a silver chair – leg over knee, talking into a telephone. He certainly looks more like David Bowie than the bleached barbie doll persona of Serious Moonlight. The hair is neatly styled to provide a characteristic quiff, delicately streaked subtle blond against natural brown.

His single-breasted, three-quarter-length jacket is the same pillar-box red as his high-waisted trousers, shirt and steel-tipped winkle pickers. Pastel shades and muted colours are out on this tour. The clothing, lights, Glass Spider and various victims wrapped in cellophane and hanging forlornly at the sides of the stage will display every pure colour of the spectrum during the concert.

Bowie completes the spoken introduction as the chair reaches the stage. He stares blankly at the audience, focusing on a point above their heads. This is rock theatre and this spider is serious stuff.

The band launch into the meat of the song – its driving rhythm heralding the start of the show proper. Bowie is on his feet, treading the boards once again.

He dives and ducks, smiling now to the audience, the red of his uniform shining like a beacon from the centre of the show. Straight into 'Day In, Day Out', no pause, no exchange – Bowie is a picture of concentration. How dear the success of this tour is to him.

At some venues, he allowed himself the luxury of speech. *"Good evening, welcome to our show. Ho, Ho."* Everything is calculated, even the spontaneity. A tight show, full of input.

The next number, also from the current album, is 'Bang Bang'.

A 'fan' is selected from the throng to collapse in giggles and awe at the sight of her 'hero'. *WE WANT TO SEE BOWIE.* He encourages her fantasies, prompting a public dance. From that moment, her dress changes from stadium-drab to stage-photogenic, and it's clear the 'fan' is, in reality, a well-rehearsed dancer. One leg over Bowie's shoulder, careful not to dislodge his walkman micro, another of Bowie's tricks. *"SHUT UP!"*

Spiderman is typically fast and precise. The song is concluded with a repudiation of the superstar's lot: *"We can't have rock stars cross-breeding with* normal *people."* Thence into 'Absolute Beginners', one of the most sweepingly grand Bowie songs of recent years, delivered with appropriate reverence.

Bowie is studied and calm and a repititious swimming mime, highlighting Bowie's understanding of the art, brings the song to a climactic conclusion.

"Hell, even at 40, this guy is impressive!", noted one observer. WE'VE SEEN BOWIE!

go through their paces and the Spider reveals its colours – the audience are clapping and shouting and Bowie is back.

More theatrics follow for the re-vamped '87 stage version of 'All The Madmen' – Bowie escorts a dancer with a wedding dress the size of a ship's sail, while *Spazz Attack* projects slides of the band in a kind of let's-fall-down-drunk manner across it. Those viewing from a distance, at this and all of Bowie's shows, gleaned nothing but confusion from most of the stage antics. The giant diamond-screens did little to alleviate the problem and perhaps, for some, only added to the frustration of not being able to see everything in detail.

The realisation of this tour was a great personal achievement for Bowie and

The crowd are awakening, pushing still, but more receptive. 'Loving The Alien', sees a blind, stumbling individual asking as many questions as posed. A true Bowie song, the singular one on 'Tonight' – it's greeted favourably – most of the audience not hearing the slightest hint of its meaning.

Still, this is a rock 'n' roll concert.

'China Girl' jolts the '83 gathering into activity. Bowie sliding across the stage in the sensual manner that is his trademark. The first real crowd-pleaser of the night.

'Fashion' sees Bowie thrown across the stage – under feet and over arms by the dancers – he's fit and knows it and even the most jaded would admit he's trying hard to entertain and impress. It's working, for when Bowie climbs up to a second-level scaffolding to scream a riotous version of 'Scary Monsters' – as the dancers

◄ Bowie '87. "I wanted this tour to have a dream-like quality", he said. "The realisation of it is certainly like a dream to me."

The 'decoy fan', supposedly pulled from the audience, metamorphosises into part of the 'Thru the Flames' dance troupe ▶

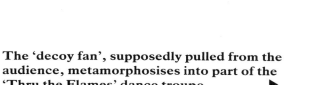

while some critics complained bitterly about the music being regarded as secondary – after so many years still ignoring Bowie's disclaimer that, by nature, he's not a total rock 'n' roller – those able to see the show clearly enjoyed it. In '87 and Cry' Bowie soared through the air to be tied up by two riot police, in 'Heroes', quite aptly, he burst free. Those once condemning Bowie for lack of movement on-stage kept quiet on this tour. He donned a white electric guitar for 'Time Will Crawl', shining against his first costume change – a sky-blue, hand-painted flying suit that made him resemble (especially against the scaffolding) a construction worker, and danced madly and freely for 'Beat Of Your Drum' and 'New York's In Love'. The real crowd mover, however, was 'Let's Dance' – the moment its pounding ascending introduction began, roars of approval erupted from the audience. Bowie spoke few words during the show, except when he wished his son, Joey, a happy 16th birthday and 60,000 people sang 'Happy Birthday'.

The show's pièce de résistance was saved for the first encore – just over two hours after the opening number.

Bowie, who once confessed to a fear of

▲   **An atmospheric moment during the 1987 revamped version of 'Big Brother'.**

39

flying, straddled the Spider to sing 'Time' – displaying golden wings to match his golden outfit, predictably wrenching the description 'angel-like' from almost every reviewer.

It was the most climactic end imaginable – people were biting their lips, holding their breath – although Bowie was singing the song with calm deliverance it looked as though the risk taken was colossal.

'Blue Jean' and 'Modern Love' brought him back down to earth and proved a fitting farewell to the show. This wasn't the David Bowie most grew accustomed to in 1983. There was no safety in numbers from familiar songs. While some sections of the press were calling this 'Bowie's last tour' – the more astute among the audience realised it marked a fresh and optimistic beginning.

After the show, Bowie and band enacted the 'getaway' – a toe-treading dash to depart the venue like quicksilver and reach the relative safety of the hotel. There would be after-show hospitality but while the minions partook of the free food and drink, Bowie was escorted, at breakneck speed, by six police bikes through the streets of Rotterdam.

For the shell-shocked crowds back at de Kuip, it would take up to two hours for some to leave the area.

Back at the Hilton, the band were chatting amiably to a small group of fans who, no doubt, spent a tiny fortune on teas and beers as they kept up their long vigil at the up-market hotel. Bowie was never glimpsed during show days – his triumph was shared only by those closest to him.

The second and final show in Rotterdam went even smoother than the first with far less nervousness on everyone's part. The plethora of props behaved themselves, certain items that malfunctioned the previous night were made to toe the line. Musically, the band were tighter and more confident – Carlos would talk to each member individually after every show and, where necessary, point out areas in their playing that could be improved.

"I don't tell the band what to do or in

▲   **The Spider reveals its colours during the show's finale**

The Flying segment from '87 & Cry' ▶

what style to play," he said. *"The most important role for a band leader is to bring out in the musicians the style and talent for which they were hired."*

The last night in Rotterdam saw a shining start to the Glass Spider tour and reluctant farewell from Bowie. *"Everyone has done so much to make us feel at home,"* he said from the stage. *"We really will be sorry to leave here."*

The tour would next move to Belgium, to play a vast outdoor venue in Werchter on June 2. That morning, and to the delight of the faithful 'Hilton scruffs', the word from the ninth floor came that Bowie would sign autographs for any fan waiting in the foyer. They were instructed to wait silently in line, which they willingly did. Until, of course, Bowie appeared and all diplomacy was thrown to the wind and a crazed mass of eager bodies surrounded the small, frail figure.

Bowie only had one bodyguard on this tour – a ramp-shouldered American equipped with eagle eyes and swivel head. *Tony Masica,* bodyguard of previous years now serves solely as his driver. Although, if the situation demanded, Masica would still provide an efficient back-up.

So Bowie left Rotterdam, swept along by a crushed tide of fans. On to the tour coach with the rest of the band, a swift acceleration and it's goodbye.

At Werchter, the weather turned foul –

wet and cold – a development that would dog almost the entire European tour. To coin a cliché, it did little to dampen people's spirits, however, and the show saw Bowie in top form.

From the acid bite of 'Scary Monsters' through to the light explosions of 'Fame' he enthralled the soaked crowds with his performance.

'87 and Cry' saw another mechanical foul-up though. Due to a malfunction of the platform that moves Bowie forward into a position to throw the ropes down to the waiting dancers, the flying segment had to be dropped.

Later, he had Erdal Kizilcay address an

◀ **Bowie's departure from Rotterdam – Mobbed by fans!**

audience for the first time in his life, got kissed by a fan who managed to steal his way onto the stage, and carried the show through to its finish in the highest of spirits. By only the third show, there was no doubt in Bowie's mind as to the ultimate success of this tour.

The fan that dashed on-stage was part of three coach-loads of English Bowie devotees that had travelled from London.

Throughout the long journey home, he talked non-stop about the experience, listening to freshly recorded tapes of the show and excitedly pointing out the precise moment of drama.

As the old adage goes, *"93 seats, 93 stories"* – and this one would bear repeated tellings for many years to come.

Press reviews of the show began to appear with increasing regularity both in Europe and Britain. Rotterdam's journalists considered that they had witnessed 'Bowie reborn' while the tabloid press in the UK all quickly ran out of adjectives to exclaim.

Only the music press, it seemed, had little praise for the show and, in particular for Bowie himself. Unlike the media overexposure of 1983, Bowie never even appeared on a music paper front cover. Reviews were small, uncomplimentary and terse. They had slammed Serious Moonlight for its predictability and

▲   **British fan Brian Jones becoming a last minute addition to the Werchter show**

largely ignored Glass Spider for whatever reason they deemed fit.

The momentum had begun, however, and bitter-bad English press would do little to halt its progress.

*   *   *

A spark of publicity would flare at the tour's next port of call – the divided city of Berlin.

1987 marked a celebration of sorts for the city – its 750th birthday and Bowie's date was part of a three-day festival of rock music commemorating the event and dubbed by its organiser, *Fritz Rau,* as "a birthday present for Berlin". The three-day 'present', two other headline acts being the *Eurythmics* and *Genesis,* was held at the Platz der Republik in front of the Reichstag and within ear-shot of East Berliners. Concerts have been held at the Reichstag (once the centre for German politics until World War II – now a museum for German history) since 1980, although until this event, had been free to the public.

As the Reichstag is extremely close to the wall, each year East Berliners would try to get as near to the frontier as possible to listen to the music drifting, unbarred, from the West. During Bowie's concert on the 6th and the following two days of the festival, their attempts this time caused scenes of rioting which created headlines all around the world.

As crowds congregated at the frontier, some even climbing on roofs to try and view the concert, the East Berlin police moved in to disperse them – heavily.

"We send our very best wishes to our friends on the other side of the wall," said Bowie during his concert – oblivious to the fighting happening out of view.

"Freedom!" and *"Down with the Wall!"* were picked up as crowd slogans by the besieged East Berliners as ultimately the police regained power and a multitude of arrests were made.

The next day, West German newspapers praised Bowie for the show and, in

Bowie als gijzelaar van zijn roeping

Spektakel met zang, muziek en dans

• Bowie aan de telefoon: „Up until one century ago…"

• David Bowie tijdens een van zijn afdalingen uit de buik van het glazen monster.

• Met plantenspuiten probeerde de ordedienst de fans koel te houden.

Stadion Feyenoord, Rotterdam: het eerste concert van de David Bowie Glass Spider Tour met David Bowie (zang, gitaar), Carlos Alomar (gitaar), …gitaar), … Pojas (bas), Erdal Kizilcay …

zend fans voelen het: de glazen spin staat op het punt te ontwaken.

Meteen de eerste verrassing als de nog onzichtbare band opent met een door vioolklanken gedomineerde, instrumentale … van Jimi Hendrix? … Een zwaar …

… pauzemuziek slag… nerveuze scanderen van zijn naam verstomt. Vijftigdui…

Slagwerkgroep … met compu…

'Bleke hertogen' als vermomming nodig heeft.

De vijf gaan wel als de me… …ende persone…

sale lijf van de spin naar beneden. Het smetteloos rood van Bowie's onberispelijke coiffure komt als laatste uit de spinnebuik gezakt.

entourage ongetwijfeld vee… zou hebben gekregen, maar in de zenuwachtige sfeer van een 'wachtkamer' wordt de… muziek toch anders ervaren. 'We will rock this house' krijgt een overmoedige miss Hendryx… …cht via de wachtenden …ergens anders: bij een …inks van het podium, …nde fans achter op …tige funk en fraaie …zang verzuipt in …olé' en 'Bowie Bo… …aar dat lijkt per de… …die een openingsact …lijk concert moet be…

…kel

… Bowie. Van meet af …alles er op dat de Glass …our haaks staat op de …k-maatstaven tradotio… …werkte Serious Moon… …mee in 1983. Het be… …heater en visuele spekta… …den gelijk al in vette klod… …ders uitgesmeerd in de openings… scène van 'Glass spider'.

Bowie daalt neer en declameert zijn boodschap sonoor in een telefoonhoorn-vormige microfoon: „Up until one century ago there lived, in the Zi Duang provence of eastern country, a glass like spider."

Een eerste zin die elementen van sprookjes en mysterie in zich draagt. Zoals zo vaak bij Bowie's teksten is het nauwelijks grijp… …melden heeft. In …

… Kizilcay steeds …s gehouden. Heel anders dan in 1983, toen verplichte kost als 'Let's dance', 'Fashion' en 'China girl' veel lichtvoetiger werd getoonzet dan nu het geval was.

Gedurfder

Ook op andere punten is deze toernee van Bowie veel gedurfder dan de voorgaande. Geheide live-successen als 'Space odditey', 'Young americans' 'Jean Genie' en zelfs 'Ziggy stardust' zijn geschrapt, omdat ze niet in het concept konden worden ingepast. Materiaal van de jongste elpee 'Never let me down' is wel rijkelijk vertegenwoordigd. Kant één wordt zelfs integraal gespeeld.

De thematiek schrijft uiteraard voor dat 'Scary monsters' een beurt krijgt. Tijdens de stevige drum- en toetsenaccenten worden de poten van de spin, die als machtige klauwen het podium in de greep houden, fel opgelicht. Op de Bühne ondersterpen de dansers de macabere sfeer van het nummer met een robbertje choreografisch vechten.

Finale

Wat wil Bowie er allemaal mee? Wat wil hij duidelijk maken? Hoe eng 'et leven kan zijn? Waarschijnlijk, want na de imposante uitvoering van 'Scary monsters' vertrouwt de verder weinig spraakzame maestro honderdduizend oren toe: 'It's rock 'n roll. She doesn't take love, she takes hostages'. Bowie als gijzelaar van zijn roeping. Zo moet het kenne…

Als hij om tien v… …afrondt met een fur… van 'Fame' trekt Bo… en even later, vo… maal, vanuit de luc… men. Hij heeft zich b… enge witte kop van de … gepoosteerd. Tegen een … vleugels spreidt hij de a… …vid Bowie als engel. Alle… …gen pianospel onderstun… tijdens een verstikkend… uitvoering van 'Time'. 'We … home by now'. Jamr… noeg, bijna.

De kop van de spin splijt op… Bowie zweeft nog eenmaal … naar het aardse. Dan is het … opsmuk af te schudden. Tijd… en finale zonder poespas… schetterende sax begeleidt Da… in 'Modern love' naar het ei… van de eerste avond wat w… geweldige wereldtoernee zal w…

Het publiek retourneert die' … met een daverende ovatie. … slotakkoorden zonder … beent over …

DAVID BOWIE

WOLFGANG NIEDECKEN.
ERASURE.
UDO LINDENBERG.
NINA HAGEN.

THE OPEN AIR …

LA DÉPÊ…

Supplément gratuit

PINSAMT AT

du Midi

SPECIAL DAVID BOWIE

Après quatre années d'absence
sur scène, un disque limité
(« Tonight »), une collaboration à
Live Aid (Wembley 85), un duo
avec Mick Jagger (« Dancing in
the street ») et un peu de cinéma
(« Absolute Beginners »), David
lk Bowie, alias David Bowie, s'est
Jones, depuis le 30 mai, dans
lancé, tentaculaire tournée mondial
six mois.

Mais pour n
l'évenemen
Bowie et de L'arar
Spider To
au Stadi
mille p
C'est p
de l'
cél
A

DAVID BOWIE

PLUS SPECIAL GUESTS BIG COUNTRY

CARDIFF ARMS PARK
SUNDAY 21st JUNE

TICKETS £15.50 (inc. 50p booking fee) Available from.

CARDIFF ARMS PARK 0222-390111	SPILLERS CARDIFF 0222-24905
SWANSEA DEREK RECORDS 0792-54226	CARDIFF HMV 0222-27147
NEWPORT ROXCENE RECORDS 0633-842656	BRISTOL HMV 0272-297467
BRIDGEND ROXCENE RECORDS 0656-59664	BIRMINGHAM ODEON 021-643 6101

SUNDERLAND ROKER PARK
TUESDAY 23rd JUNE

TICKETS £15.50 (inc 50p booking fee) Available from:

SUNDERLAND ROKER PARK 091-514 0332	NEWCASTLE HMV 0632-327470
NEWCASTLE CITY HALL 091-261 2606	EDINBURGH HMV 031-226 3466
MIDDLESBROUGH HMV 0642 226957	DURHAM VIRGIN 0385 65850
GLASGOW VIRGIN RECORDS 041-226 4679	YORK VIRGIN RECORDS 0904-647441
MIDDLESBROUGH NEW HOUSE MUSIC 0642-247314	

utmärkt gitarrist. Men han saknar
riktig originalitet, han fick för
äntligen en   mycket plats på **Carlos Alomars**
bekostnad och han har inte ett uns
mest ade-   av den råhet och skärpa som **Earl
Slick** hade på sin tid.

Iggy Pop då?
Jodå, denna utseendemässiga
och plastiska korsning mellan
Niels Jensen och **Susanne Lane-
feldt** och osannolike dödspolare
med Bowie gjorde bra ifrån sig
med rykande "Blah blah" och
"Raw power".
Urpunk som faktiskt lät bättre
på Eriksberg än på Draken i
Stockholm i hostas.
Nig-och-jucka-runt utan fem-
tielva dansare.
Maktig intensitet som i "Win-
ners and losers" utan flummiga
ramhandlingar, obegripliga ba-
lettutflykter och stora rekvisita-
förråd.
Annat skulle det bli lite senare.

Utstuderat fjantigt

Och när David Bowie efter nära
två timmars offbroadwaykör inle-
der sina extranummer gör han det
i konsekvensens namn på ett
minst lika utstuderat fjantigt sätt
som tidigare.
Han sjunger "Time" ståande på
dammsug . . . förlåt . . . spindelns
huvud med vingar av guld . . . JO,
JAG LOVAR . . . som FLAXAR!
Allt detta, gott folk, "för att" —
om man får tro upphovsmannen —
"ställa frågan om rocken har
någon mening längre".
"Och hur den i så fall ska få
tillbaka sin mening."
Vi kan diskutera "Glass Spider"-satsningen tills korna kom-
mer hem.
Vi kan analysera, dividera och

HARVEY GOLDSMITH PROUDLY PRESENTS

SOUNDS April 18 1987 Page 5

THE GLASS SPIDER TOUR

WEMBLEY
TICKETS £16.50
(inc 50p booking fee)
Tickets available by post from
DAVID BOWIE WEMBLEY
P.O. Box 77 London SW4 5LH
Cheques/ Postal orders ONLY payable to
David Bowie Box Office
Allow 28 days for delivery & Enclose S.A.E
IN ASSOCIATION WITH SOLO

CARDIFF ARMS PARK
TICKETS £15.50 (inc 50p booking fee)
Available from.

SUNDERLAND
TICKETS £15.50 (inc 50p booking fee)
Available from.

CREDIT CARD HOTLINE 01-788 1818
(SUBJECT to Agency Booking fee)

ing tillbaka. Men musikaliskt får han godkänt
Foto: PAUL HANSEN

CIRCU

● David Bow
houdt van sl
theater, ma
van circus.
Daarom kock
popster gewo
een kaartje br
VVV en ging n
de Rotterdam
première van
circus Mullens
Bowie, die
zaterdag en
zondag in de Ku
de eerste
concerten geeft
van zijn

wereldtoernee, z
er echter niet
lekker rustig. De
zanger werd
voortdurend
belaagd door
vooral jeugdig

particular his cordial greeting to the East. A city always sympathetic to Bowie, in 1977 Berlin became his own personal place of refuge from the angst-ridden world of rock – where an exorcism of drugs and personality disorder was performed and where realistic long-term perspectives were gained. A decade later, Berlin saw a healthy, clear-minded David Bowie while he viewed a torn city with the dividing gulf yawning ever wider.

On June 7, the Glass Spider tour reached Nurberg Rock AM festival, a massive, sprawling affair located discreetly in the German countryside – a respectable hour-long drive from the country's capital, Bonn.

Thousands upon thousands attended this show – camped out in clusters, swarming around the plentiful beer tents and maintaining a staunch vigil at the front of Bowie's stage. Five hours before Bowie performed, the audience were already half-crushed, soaking wet and party to a constant' stream of air-less bodies that were hauled over shoulders to the security men in front of the stage. When you're

caught in such a mass crowd the only way out is forward. Behind you stands a veritable ocean of biology – the same either side. If some over-eager, or over-mean individual decides to start pushing way back, the domino theory, backed by the weight of a million limbs, comes into play. Rock concerts, given the right atmosphere can be great fun, but often they bring out the worst in people who consider they have a god-given right to the best view and woe betide any lesser mortal that may bar their way.

Bowie's show began around 10.30pm which meant an awful lot of exhausted people watching, so the crowds began to become less desperate and more intent on enjoying the spectacle.

The double-stadium sized field was ablaze with sparklers for many portions of the show – a progression from the lighter/ matches tradition – and Bowie gave a receptive and lively performance. He still finds it difficult to talk to an audience in anything other than perfunctory terms, although, throughout his entire career, that has never been a key factor in his shows.

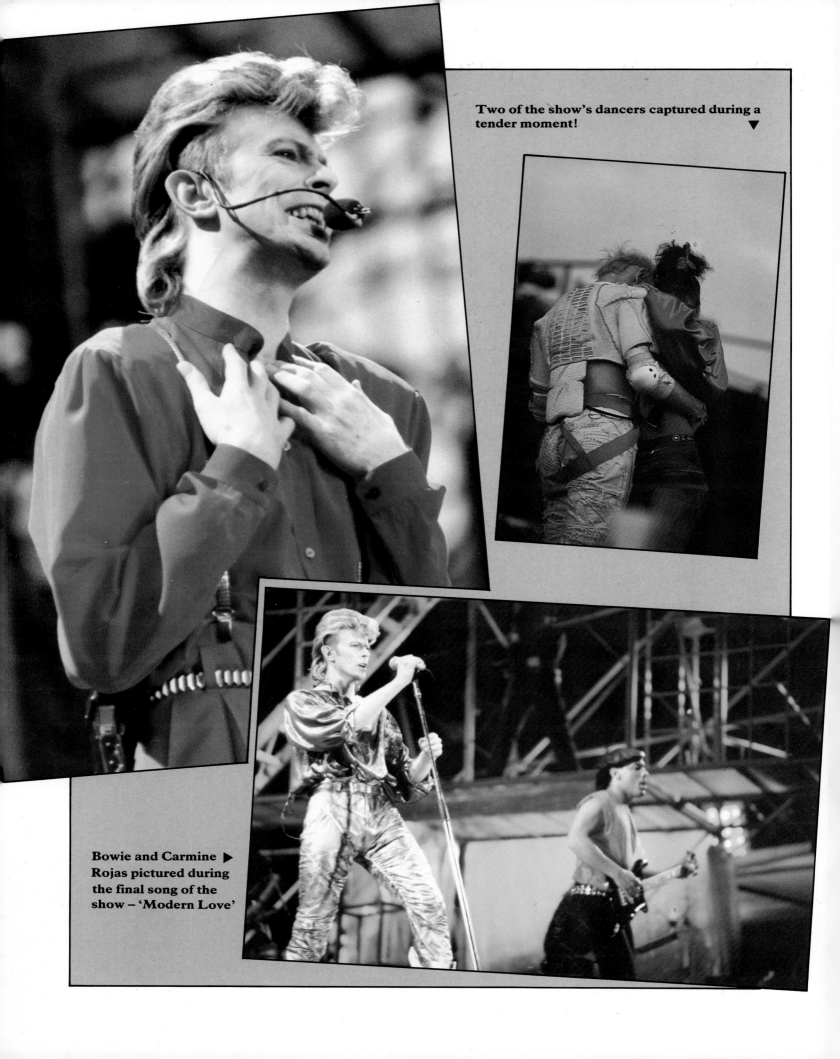

Two of the show's dancers captured during a tender moment! ▼

Bowie and Carmine ▶ Rojas pictured during the final song of the show – 'Modern Love'

Following the descent of '87 & Cry.'

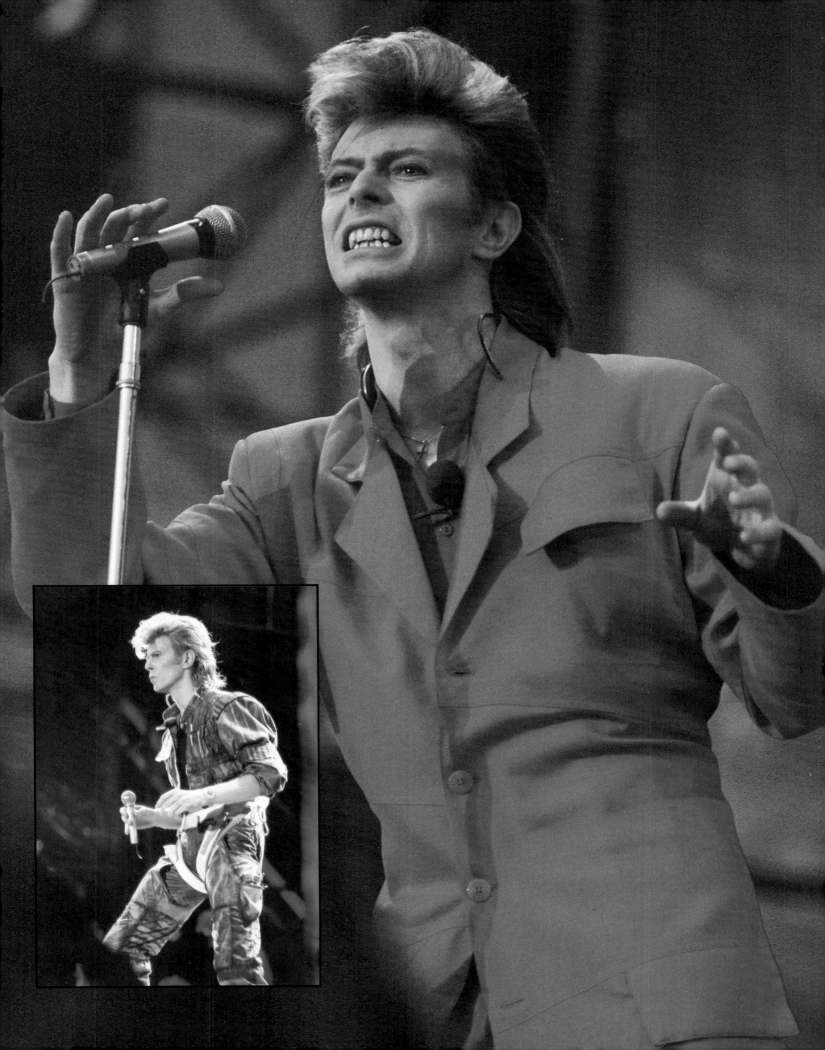

THE GLASS SPIDER T

PHOT

RECTANGLE

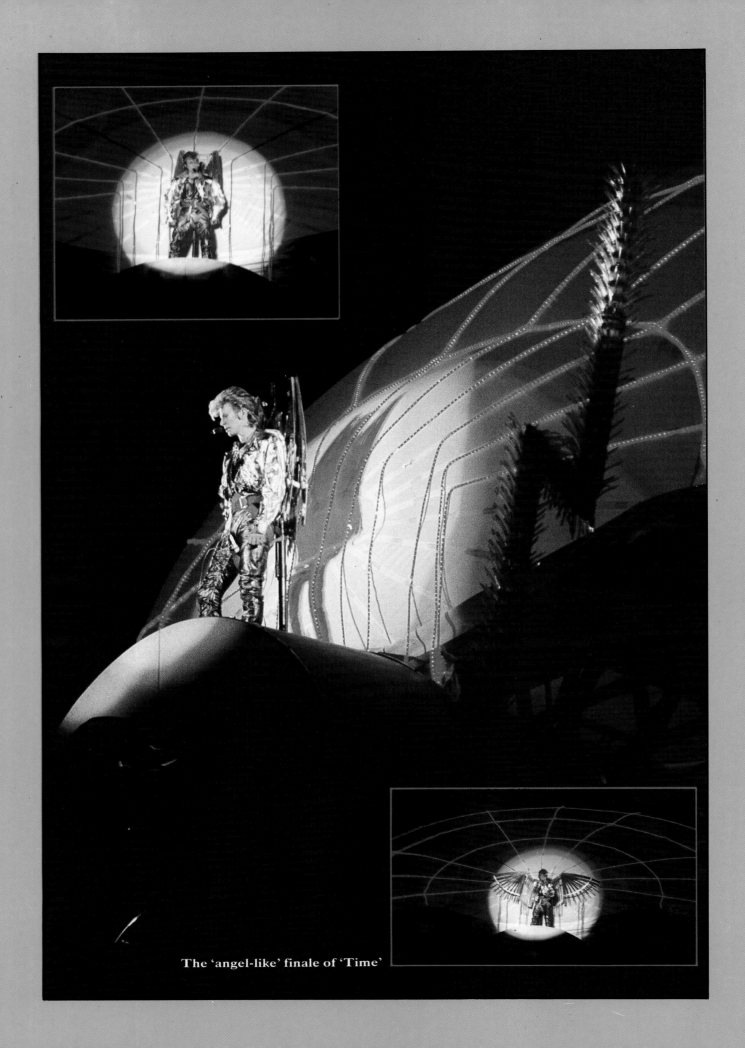

The 'angel-like' finale of 'Time'

The tour one week old, 23 to go, and I began collecting opinions from concert-goers and, more specifically, from a wide section of 'knowledgeable' fans. But first, consider the dilemma of such an individual as David Bowie: Over 20 years in the business, assembling a huge catalogue of recordings, many tagged 'influential' or 'pure genius' or 'innovative' and a fame all-enveloping.

While other artists, those eligible to boast such longevity if not the initial *intense* adulation, can remain unscathed because they simply make good records – Bowie has always been expected to offer much more.

Certainly his face alone has contributed to his much-touted legend. Not everyone could recite the lyrics to 'Width Of A Circle' or would want to, but nearly everyone knows that David Bowie has different coloured eyes, gets a new haircut every week and sometimes has the reputation of looking like a girl.

It would be no lie to observe that Bowie has been responsible for a good 40 per cent of 'rock looks' over the last 15 years, although, contrary to popular belief, he's hardly been aware of it. So, after four years, he decides to tour again. How would he choose the songs from the hundreds he's written? In what new guise shall he appear to enthral the masses?

Citing from the laws of probability, it's inevitable that whatever kind of show he enacts, many people are bound to be disappointed that he didn't play 'Space Oddity' or 'Drive-In Saturday' or 'Sound And Vision'.

All that aside, the majority of reactions gleaned were enthusiastically favourable – many considering that Bowie was staging a fan's tour in the older tradition rather than the newer one.

Some said that the show contained too much recent material and yearned for songs from the Ziggy era (although, in my judgement, Bowie's finale of 'Time' is a direct descendant of those days). Others found some moments 'too theatrical' for a rock show.

Bowie fans are certainly among the most devoted and opinionated and hundreds would follow this tour all across Europe despite their statements.

"We wouldn't like fans to think that we've no concern for their thoughts," offered Carlos Alomar on the subject. *"All of us, especially David have great respect for the fans and like to encourage them. Most of them just want to meet David to say 'thanks' and that's appreciated."*

Florence, Italy, was the next dot on the map for the Glass Spider tour – notable for the fact that the concert, on June 9, marked the very first time Bowie had played a show in the country. History buffs may point out that Bowie had played (and won) an Italian song festival in 1969, but that solo number would hardly constitute a concert and was definitely not viewed by 70,000 people.

Earlier in the year, during the press conference tour, Bowie and entourage were mobbed at Rome airport. Sheer

pandemonium ensued at the realisation of his intentions, for this meant the first time ever for Italian fans who are, rest assured, plentiful in numbers.

The Florence date was marred with tragedy, however, 90 minutes before Bowie was due to take the stage, a lighting engineer fell 75ft from the scaffolding and suffered multiple injuries from the fall.

The British engineer, *Michael Clark* had worked on previous Bowie shows since 1978 and the singer wept when he heard the news.

A member of the road crew said: *"He considered cancelling the concert because he was so upset but finally decided to go through with the show as a mark of respect. Michael suffered appalling injuries and everyone was deeply shaken up."*

In Milan, trouble also struck, though not so close to home, as swarming crowds of Italian fans, unable to obtain tickets for Bowie's show at Milan soccer stadium, became restless and started throwing stones and even fireworks into the stadium. The police charged in and eventually, to avoid further trouble, the mob were allowed, minus tickets, into the venue.

In Hamburg, Bowie made headlines for a meeting with Danish royalty as he greeted *Prince Joachim* and *Crown Prince Frederik* backstage at Stadt Park, before that night's concert.

The young princes were self-confessed admirers of the singer, and the meeting was arranged as an 18th birthday present for Prince Joachim by one of Germany's largest daily newspapers.

Press reports covering the meeting were decidedly infantile with one in particular writing: *"The princes were rather self-conscious when they stood face to face with David Bowie and he was visibly honoured at becoming a royal rock star. But before you could say 'Jack Robinson' they had hit it off and were having an animated conversation on rock. Joachim said that he was impressed by Bowie's talent for changing his style, which warmed the cockles of Bowie's heart."* Indeed.

LOCAL HERO

On June 19 and 20, David Bowie returned to London to stage two concerts at Wembley Stadium, the scene of his triumph at Live Aid two years previously.

The Wembley shows were the first tour dates to be announced and tickets for the massive venue had sold out months before. What wasn't so predictable was the weather.

1987 saw the wettest June for many years and the first of Bowie's shows at the stadium was dogged by torrential rain, causing the field to turn to mud despite the covering, and leaving the punters clutching water-logged programmes.

"This must be the Seriously Soaking tour," said one, obviously undeterred concert-goer.

Some laughed, some screamed but most kept quiet and prayed for the sun to be the 'special guest' promised on the tickets.

As well as the usual selection of tour t-shirts and merchandise, the stalls were also selling 'body bags' – clear plastic coverings – for 10p. An awful lot were sold.

Unbeknown to the great well-and-truly-washed, Bowie and entourage had been resident at the London Hilton two days prior to the Wembley shows and had already undergone a number of sound-checks at the stadium.

While in London, on June 18, Bowie visited the BBC Top Of The Pops studios and taped a special performance of his then current single 'Time Will Crawl' for screening at a later date.

This was the first time Bowie had sung live for the show since 1977 when he performed 'Heroes' and, in an extreme case of short-sightedness, even when the single moved slightly up the charts, the recording was never screened. The TOTP controller was more willing to give time to Top Ten acts. It wouldn't take much guesswork to surmise that it would be a long time before Bowie ever gave the show anything like that again. Perhaps someone should have told them that

Stephen Nichols eyes Bowie before the manhandling sequences of 'Fashion'

PART FOUR

68

David Bowie *rarely* gives live television performances.

In recent interviews, Bowie had been commenting, bitterly, about the page three models splashed across the national press. Not about the girls specifically but about . . . *"What surrounds the photographs. The rape stories and innuendo of violence against sex laid side by side. I find it unbelievably offensive when it's done in such a titillating manner."*

For the TOTP performance Bowie wore a jacket with page three type pictures emblazoned across each shoulder.

Looking ahead, he arrived at the studio with 'Censored' stickers, assuming the floor manager would take one look at his garb and flatly refuse to allow him to wear it. Much to the singer's astonishment, nothing was said and the recording went ahead without any protests.

Later the same night, the stickers came into use for the benefit of photographers who had stalked Bowie out at the Café de Paris and snapped him with model *Marie Helvin* as they departed in the early hours.

The next morning, the day of the first Wembley show, most papers carried the

photographs along with the revelation that Bowie and Helvin were *'an item.'*

What every news-hound forgot to point out, and which every picture editor conveniently cropped, was the fact that Marie Helvin was not only in the company of David Bowie but also, there on her other arm but mysteriously absent in every reproduction, her fiancé.

Such gossip creates publicity, however, and, although not in the most scrupulous manner, it served to announce that David Bowie was back in town with the Glass Spider road show lumbering along behind him.

The first of the Wembley dates was not the finest show of the tour. By this time, he had dropped 'New York's In Love' from the set and, on this occasion, also dropped the stunning finale of 'Time'. Weather conditions dictated this move, as it would at future concerts. Too much rain, too much wind and Bowie's perch would become genuinely perilous.

As the foul weather continued, it would develop into a wait-and-see game at future shows which left many people disappointed but also added to the thrill when

Glass
idol

During the second half of the show – Bowie's ▶
first costume change

conditions were kind. At any rate, Wembley first night was a smooth, successful yet less animated show, Bowie offered only curt comments to the audience (*"It's good to be back."*) and went through the motions without any great feeling.

On past tours, insiders have noted that David develops a nervousness before playing to a home crowd. During his London press conference, Bowie had said: *"The London dates will be extremely important to me. When you're born in a place – that becomes the big one."*

Whether that nervousness still exists is unknown, and it would be pure assumption of me to say otherwise, but it is a fact that, on this tour as on others, Bowie's first night in town is always more stilted than subsequent nights.

After the show, Bowie and band congregated at the West End night-spot Legends for a private party that lasted well into Saturday morning. The show's dancers commanded the dance floor for most of the night, with David occasionally joining them for a high-spirited dance.

The next day, next show, next ticket stub, saw a transformed Bowie perform an energetic, emphatic show to another sea of people.

One vast difference between this tour and the Serious Moonlight tour, apart from the obvious, is the wider and more controlled range of Bowie's voice. Unlike '83, Bowie's pitch reaches much higher and thus affords more 'faithful' renditions of his songs. Even the closing song, 'Modern Love' is delivered with more harmonic power than its '83 counterpart –

▲ **Carlos and Peter Frampton compare riffs**

Glass idol

◀ **Sporting the briefly used white electric guitar during 'Time Will Crawl'**

'Fame' also provided a final opportunity for Bowie to include the audience and the song was shortened or lengthened individually at each concert, depending on crowd reaction.

Bowie's second Wembley date did include 'Time', enthralling all including *Princess Diana* in the royal box, who had attended and danced constantly at both dates, and, according to past press reports had asked specifically to meet only David Bowie at Live Aid.

Bowie's last night in London was spent, in the company of *Mick Jagger*, at Bill Stickers – a fashionable restaurant in Soho that boasts imaginative decor complete with dancers gyrating in cages suspended from the ceiling.

Press reviews of the concerts were unanimously unfavourable, continuing a press trend determined not to find a good word to say about anything. Whether such criticism affected Bowie is unknown, but it is doubtful considering his knowledge of the whims of the press and the bias that surrounds such journalism.

Meanwhile, the pack of unofficial t-shirt sellers had moved into newer pastures and begun, in various market stalls in the city, to sell bootlegged cassette tapes of the concerts.

The winner of the 'bare-faced cheek' award, however, must go to one trader in Brick Lane market who attempted to sell bottles of 'Bowie Air'.

For £1 you could have a bottle containing "actual air breathed out by Bowie at Wembley '87". A vital addition to any collection. To the street traders that ply their hastily-produced wares outside stadiums, it matters little to them who or what the subject matter is – as long as the crowds are there. A stolen logo, faded photograph and the golden words '1987 Tour' are all that's needed to convince spell-bound attendants that the merchandise is desirable. Fake programmes, fake tour shirts all combined with the originals on the backs of the audience. For himself,

then it was little more than a hoarse scream.

This fact alone goes some way to describing the state of Bowie's health and the sheer dedication applied to making the show work. Despite the criticism levelled against the format of the show, few could disagree that Bowie's voice was performing at peak condition.

Especially on June 20, when Bowie relaxed and delivered a vintage concert, fuelled by the applause, screams and whistles of 70,000 people. Songs that were rapidly becoming fervent crowd-pleasers in the 'Let's Dance' vein included 'All The Madmen', 'Absolute Beginners' and, not surprisingly, 'Fame' which, as its highlight offered a synchronised dance routine with all four dancers, culminating with a collective 'charging bull' segment that Bowie had previously used for 'Jean Genie'.

David Bowie's...
tomorrow... playing
...hum interview

WESTERN MAIL

THE NATIONAL NEWSPAPER OF WALES · PAPUR CENEDLAETHOL CYMRU

No 36,637   23p

90-DAY NOTICE
SHARES
8.05% 11.03%
92 St Mary...
Telephone (0222) 27328

Monday, June 22, 1987 ★★

TODAY

BOWIE IN CARDIFF

PICTURE SPECIAL — Page 5

BOWIE'S NEW GIRL BOWS IN

● ROCK idol David Bowie was giving nothing away after being spotted with a new date in London's West End. Even her name was a riddle ... just Johnson, he said.

● As the two strolled arm-in-arm in Piccadilly Circus, Bowie quipped: "Now I'll be accused of leading her astray to a life of sex, drugs and rock n' roll."

● Not surprisingly the lady was looking none too pleased. For after a quick goodnight kiss the singer left her to go out on the town

Bowie the winner as touts are foiled

By NEIL JONES

CONCERT TICKET touts' hopes of cashing in on rock superstar David Bowie's visit to Cardiff suddenly put on sale another 2,000 tickets.

As the afternoon wore on prices tumbled from a "high" of double the £15 face value to about £10 in many street-corner salesmen.

The concert was a massive success as the capital city and thousands of adoring Bowie fans basked in Midsummer's Day sunshine.

Police reported little trouble and organisers of the National Stadium concert were celebrating what they hoped would be just the first in a series of rock extravaganzas.

Seven people were charged with offences including assault, deception, drugs session and drunkenness outside for parking offences and traffic violations, but a police spokesman said early today. "In general the crowd was very well-behaved."

Ticket dealers had arrived from all over the country for the day, with one even flying over from West Germany to follow the superstar's roadshow.

Many of the touts were Londoners, and most were also involved in selling T-shirts, sweat-shirts, head bands and souvenirs.

"Another batch of tickets went on sale first thing in the morning, so this meant a considerable dent in the expected profits for the touts," said a salesman for the Harvey Goldsmith promoters.

There were no reports of fake tickets in circulation and one salesman, who came clearly out to spot any that could have slipped the net.

Concert security staff were also out in force — often outnumbering police on the ground.

"The money has really been made in T-shirts and other souvenirs," said one salesman. "We've learned all the tricks from our trips selling scarves at rugby matches and we know the area well.

"The security have tried to warn us off, but because we've been selling gear at half the official price we have done very well. "It's only the tickets that have let us down."

Others bought profits from the day included off-licences, quick-food vendors and the city's publicans who have benefited greatly by selling six-packs of lager from 75p, but on the whole businesses resisted the temptation of raising prices.

One burger bar bought sausages 2,000 burgers just for pop fans and many of the bars sold hundreds of cans and bottles during afternoon opening hours.

More pictures — Page 5

Picture by PAUL ROSE

● David Bowie in full voice last night.

How Ziggy fell to earth

MAGIC MASTER DAVID OPENS WORLD TOUR IN TRIUMPH

DAILY EXPRESS Monday June 1 1987

Spiderman Bowie spins a web of wonder

SEVENTY thousand fans from all over Europe were drawn into David Bowie's "Glass Spider" web. And even those who paid ten times over the £18 entrance fees went away believing they had been touched by magic.

The master showman's multi-million pound show which opened his world tour at Rotterdam on Saturday night defied the imagination at times, apparently gravity and logic.

Under a huge inflatable spider draped on the stage, Bowie soared above the Feyenoord stadium, the city's football ground in a bewildering blend of bridges wizardry and symbolism.

The exhausting two-hour performance opened with Bowie descending from a cord inside the spider, telephone on a silver dining, telephone on a silver as he climaxed with him portraying a shimmering silver angel, standing on top of the spread creature.

Sensational

In between, the rock millionaire fed his audience begged for further sensational dance and gymnastic routines. Later as touring after his return Bowie who has been fascinated by years...

From ROGER TAVENER in Rotterdam

nervous. At the same time hell, it's only rock and roll and does my head in and I don't know whether I will ever be able to tour anything this complicated again.

For me this is a coming together and is theatrical performance that have married up working elements into my working impact, but I also want colourful rock.

The Glass Spider was certainly all of those actor, the crowd always turned on. My latest album are tracks which include most of before his 25 year one about among but did favourite store the 25 performances alternate Time Fashion show Absolute beginners and lighting crowd on the Sunderland...

DAVID BOWIE
THE GLASS SPIDER TOUR

SPECIAL GUEST

IGGY POP

ERIKSBERG – GÖTEBORG – 27 JUNI – 1987

Fabulous web of spiderman Bowie

From GARRY BUSHELL in Holland

HE'S BEEN the Thin White Duke, Aladdin Sane and Ziggy Stardust.

But when David Bowie launched his latest world tour he was something completely different.

On Saturday night I watched Bowie open his Glass Spider show, the most theatrical Diamond Dogs trek in 1974.

And not so frenzied fans saw it with...

The sell-out concert at sized Feyenoord Stadium was that Rotterdam's Wembly dum and was first night of a mammoth tour that will take in more than 100 cities in more than six months over the next months.

Outside touts were flogging tickets were going for as much as £100 come from far away as the USA and Japan by Bowie's first live show since Live Aid in 1985 and crowd was expected...

It was some 560,000 petrol amazing 580,000 and two world metals drink drinks tour hundred mile for nearly 1,400,000 million...

The only time he slowed go into action when he sang Happy Birthday to his band the six-man round he won tighter band they were get with defence and accuracy Peter Frampton a dazzling double lead dancers who were at as musical routines were sinister version of drowning Brother.

Monsters But as greater mundane the Dance usual replay. Bowie threw in 'some album which includes a of routine sister...

red Ted to a cosmic cowboy with a blue back as a winged angel number. Time only moan you needed binoculars to watch the action — there was so much happening the giant video screen couldn't keep up.

But nothing outshone Bowie. He may be 40 but he was the fittest man on stage which two-hour show which included doses of Me Down, Day I Never Let Me Down, Wayne Scene the excitement of that Zeroes Day.

Fans jumped on their seats and boogied as Bowie ripped through classy numbers funky like Dance Fame and Modern Love.

At they say in his old South London stomping ground, Bowie business, let him back...

Pictures: DAVE HRGAR

LET'S DANCE   Bowie boogies with a beauty

THE GLASS SPIDER TOUR

THE IRISH TIM

Price 55p incl. VAT
50p sterling area

FRIDAY, JULY 10, 1987

VIE The Glass Spid Tou

David Bowie is surrounded by young fans on his arrival at Dublin Airport yesterday for his Slane concert tomorrow. — (Photograph: Pat Langan)

PR men riled, but Bowie smiled

By Ronan Fjister

DA'ID BOWIE doesn't own Dublin Airport, it just looked that way when he arrived yesterday on a Ryanair jet from Barcelona for the concert at Slane, Co. Meath tomorrow.

Even before his plane touched down, Bowie's advance public relations man ended up in a countretemps with newspaper photographers over just who could and not go out

Joe Breen profiles David Bowie: page 10

onto the tarmac to see the megastar step off the plane.

al tour comes to Britain. so nights at Wembley s by Bryan Appleyard

Bowie's high spot

HOTLIPS: Marie and the star who censored himself.
Pictures: KEITH BUTCHER

Bowie's go

OUT on the town with a beautiful woman, rock star David Bowie had plenty to talk about.

He cuddled up to model Marie Helvin — photographer David Bailey's ex — and announced:

"I'll be taking Marie off into a life of sin, sex and debauchery on the streets of the world."

Then, having said ore than a gallant ort ought to, he sen-

sibly covered his mouth with a sticky strip reading 'censored'.

The couple, who were leaving a London nightspot together, are both divorced.

Were they truly now thinking of linking up? David, who appears at Wembley tonight, wouldn't say.

His lips were sealed. But friends reckon it was all just another of his gags.

● White Hot Club—Page 13

in Ireland, he said.

A night ou with model Marie—say no more . .

★ THIS is the moment which has had pop fans across Europe holding their breath as David Bowie appears, angel-like, on top of the 50ft-high fibre-glass spider for his encore on his current 100-date world tour. Fans at Wembley tonight will see the spider during Bowie's two-hour set.

Bowie daalt af in (Kuip) stoeltje

★ Het begin van de wereldtournee van David Bowie. Terwijl hij het nummer Glass Spider inluidt, zakt superster van de pren scremig in het Feyenoordstadion uit de overkapping van het podium naar bene- den.

Bij het concert werden zaterdag avond negen jongelui gearresteerd wegens openbaarheid aan drugs en spelde- overtreding. Van de negen 17 er messen dan 25 ticket af merken grond en niesen ranklen grond en zich later behandeld gens kappersintdis

De politie spant in rushas reisin Tseblus is gotvanlom de 19 aan, gidvoorran en bevalt verzen te uit Polka B & S hue de

Op pagina's s Bowie speelt het handig

HIS FINAL TOUR — AND A BRAND NEW LOOK

Rock

A last tango with Bowie . . .

by LESLEY-ANN JONES
IN ROTTERDAM

IT WAS vintage Fred Astaire. g Col Charisse. A wild-eyed Gabli lauer's seemingly endless ige drape a... broad left shoulder, rock millio over his David Bowie is back...

Changing faces: Ziggy (left), in Absolute Beginners, and (right) Bowie dancing on stage at the weekend

Colour poster inside

Special 20p

◀ **The Golden Chameleon – the third costume change for the stunning encores**

player *Richard Cottle*, Swansea born and bred, the Cardiff show was a special day for him, and his family, making the journey from Swansea, were in attendance to share it with him.

After the concert, police praised the "excellent behaviour" of the crowd and, along with the organisers and every drink and food seller in the area, hoped the success of the Bowie show would enable the venue to stage summertime concerts regularly in the future.

For one fan, the Cardiff date saw a culmination of adoration that reached back to 1972 when Bowie first unleashed his carrot-topped Ziggy Stardust to the rock world.

Kay Waliker, 43, claimed that Bowie was a regular caller at a flower shop where she worked in that year in Monmouth, adding that he lived for a time in nearby Ross-on-Wye while using the nearby Rockfield recording studios.

"He was so pleasant in those days that I started following him," she said. *"It really is a dream come true to see him play Cardiff."*

After playing Sunderland on June 23, Bowie made a return visit to London to attend a children's charity lunch and auction, and also to accept an award from the charity for his unpublicised work on their behalf.

During the auction, Bowie paid £15,000 for an *Everly Brothers* guitar – proudly posing for photographers with the instrument before promptly handing it back, enabling the charity to sell it again the following year, effectively giving the charity a £30,000 donation.

His award was given to him by the *Duchess of York,* who had wined and dined with the singer earlier in the evening and confessed to him that, like her royal counterpart the Princess of Wales, she was also a great admirer of his music.

Pushing onwards, the tour reached Gothenburg, on June 27 to play a venue at Eriksberg, organised swiftly in a panic

but also for others, David Bowie is a walking, money-making machine and each year the traders become more organised, create more merchandise and cart away more tax-free, royalty-free money.

Traders did well in Cardiff – the next date of the tour as the city staged its first ever stadium concert at the Arms Park Rugby ground.

The Glass Spider tour marked a series of firsts for Bowie and Cardiff was the latest in line drawing an impressive 50,000 fans from all over the UK. *"It's hard to believe that someone like David Bowie has finally decided to come to Cardiff,"* enthused one local fan. *"I think it's proved that a visit like this has been long overdue."*

For once, the show was blessed with blue skies and the Welsh crowds responded with appropriate vigour. For keyboard

◀ **Second-storey scaffolding for 'Scary Monsters'**

after the original venue, the Ullevi Stadium banned Bowie because the damage bill after a concert by *Bruce Springsteen* came to £2.7 million. By now, local press were polishing their act, and reports of Bowie's activities in Gothenburg however incidental, were published with great relish. Swedish fans were informed that Bowie stayed in his hotel room for much of the time while band members went shopping. He reached Eriksberg by boat across a river and commented on how pleasant the crossing was. At the concert, he watched *Iggy Pop* on-stage – the support for the show – and even managed a brief chat with his friend before taking to the stage himself.

On the mainland, the Swedish press informs its readers that, after the show Bowie is relaxed and walks with an arm around a band member back to his hotel. He dines later with Iggy, signs a few autographs for a contingent of fans who've waited diligently for 72 hours outside the hotel and comments to waiting hacks that *"The concert was definitely the warmest so far on this tour."*

The show reviews, however, displayed no awed reverence and, while most critics found praise for Iggy's set, hammered nails of animosity into the back of Bowie's skull.

One reviewer said: *"Bowie has simply smashed his blonde head into the wall of the pretentious end of a cul-de-sac. If this is the way rock music is going to get back its meaning, the answer is no."*

Praise and criticism for Bowie seems to come in very methodical waves. On this tour, it was most definitely in vogue to consider Bowie unfashionable and write copy accordingly.

By the time the tour reached Paris, however, the show was getting into gear and had developed into a tight, powerful and confident entity. The Paris show, at the Park de la Courneuze – another lush green setting for Boris the Spider to crouch in, was held on July 3 – a gloriously hot summer's day, offering respite from what was proving to be a real bad weather tour. The French took David Bowie to their hearts many years ago, picking up more on his classic elegance and authentic use of high fashion – something the Parisians adore as a matter of national course. Bowie had played Toulouse the previous night, successfully, and his mood was buoyant as he took to the Paris stage.

A high-spirited David Bowie delivers a memorable concert – the singer relaxes into songs and, quite often, punctuates them with unrehearsed lines and comments. He moves and dances with abandon, less consciously so, and communicates with the audience that, he too,

can enjoy the atmosphere offered by a rock concert.

"Are you lot doing anything later?" he quizzed the crowds at Paris. *"No? Well, we'll carry on then."*

'Heroes' was ecstatic, 'Beat Of Your Drum' moved limbs and the encores were each greeted with deafening applause. A major advantage European concerts have over their British equivalents is that no curfew exists stipulating the time the show must start and finish. Ergo, European shows start later in suitable light conditions that ensure the light show is viewed as intended – bright, colourful and commanding attention. Indoor venues don't have this problem, but in stadiums, during the long British summer evenings, too many distractions exist for a concert to function at maximum capacity.

Bowie grew increasingly thinner as the tour progressed ▶

Entering into new territory, and returning, surprisingly enough to the bad weather trend, the tour moved from France to Spain – to play three concerts in Madrid and Barcelona. It was during these concerts that Bowie decided to relent to pressure and add a couple of 'standard' numbers to the set. He dropped 'Zeroes' and lengthened the show further by adding 'Jean Genie', 'Young Americans' and 'White Light, White Heat'. Due to the band size, the '87 versions of these songs, specifically the raw, thudding riff of 'Jean Genie' – prefaced with organ music and an invitation from Bowie to *"Go to church"*, were louder and more rock orientated than on the last tour. Audience reaction proved that the decision was a wise one.

On July 11, the Glass Spider tour played Slane Castle in County Meath, Ireland – yet another premiere performance from Bowie. Press coverage centred around another tragedy however – the death of *Sean Smith*, a 20-year-old fan who drowned in the River Boyne, which runs around the festival site, while trying to enter the backstage area. A similar death occurred when Bob Dylan played Slane three years previously, and the incident at Bowie's show coupled with reports of stabbings, marred the event. Attendance was below expectations for the Slane concert – drawing 50,000 in an area that could have housed at least another 20,000. Throughout the concert, which was performed in total daylight – the local authorities demanded the show end at 9pm – the crowds were pushing heavily, prompting Bowie to stop singing a couple of times and tell the front rows to ease up.

"We didn't come here to see people getting legs and arms broken," he said.

Later that evening, the star dined with Peter Frampton at Dublin's Casper and Giumbini's and offered a few random thoughts to the ever-present journalists:

"Slane was like a holiday. The place is great and the crowd were responsive. There was one moment when I thought the crowd looked dangerous and I had to tell them to stop pushing, but it's been wonderful to be in Ireland."

A few days' rest and then the tour wound its way to the city of Manchester – final two British dates and a collective reunion of sorts for the country-hopping 'superfans', many of whom had followed the tour passionately since its Rotterdam première. Between their varied exploits a veritable swop-shop of thoughts and experiences ensued – each an individual story of one person's Bowie tour.

By now, through familiarity and justifying their expense, all considered the Glass Spider tour to be the best Bowie had ever undertaken. They'd seen the mistakes, the omissions, the additions and had witnessed first-hand a theatrical show gradually take shape and solidify into something unique. *"Yes"*, they all agreed, *"It had all been worthwhile."*

For his Manchester shows, Bowie rewarded such devotion with two nights of pure entertainment. I was particularly taken, by the vast difference between these and previous concerts.

The audience rejoiced at 'Jean Genie', and the ending of 'Fame' was lengthened for an eternity with an ad-libbing Bowie interjecting versions of 'London Bridge Is Falling Down', 'War' and, oddly enough, 'Who Will Buy?'.

"I've suffered for Fame", he screeched, emphatically as the audience, an unshakeable by-product of fame, prompted him to go ever further.

Then it's goodbye to Boris, the final British bow and the veiled promise from Bowie that *"We will be back."*

During off-duty nights in Manchester, Bowie and band held private parties in the bar of the New Midland hotel, before going on to a club named Applejacks where scrambled eggs cost a staggering £35!

A week-long holiday was planned after the final European show in Nice, securely hidden from prying eyes on a private beach, before the Glass Spider tour would inch its way to America.

Bowie left Europe, having played a total of 27 concerts to an average of over a million people, across 13 countries over two months.

He'd been idolised, praised, slammed, ridiculed and even exalted. While Serious Moonlight found almost universal favour, this tour split opinions savagely, separating the casual Bowie fan from the dyed-in-the-wool fanatic.

If Bowie's main intention with the tour was to re-establish himself as a performance artist, illustrating that his future career is not quite as predictable as some might believe, then he succeeded.

His past still hangs heavily around his neck, often distorting people's perceptions of present work. A building up of expectations, a face-blank refusal to consider him anything other than a talented artist.

Bowie's Glass Spider tour saw a new-found willingness to take chances and push boundaries further – proving his own publicity that states: 'As always, the way for David Bowie is forever forward.'

The road may not always be smooth and direct, but David Bowie is most certainly firmly on course.

TECHNICAL DETAILS

PART FIVE

THE EUROPEAN GLASS SPIDER TOUR ITINERARY

Press Conferences

MARCH
17 **TORONTO,** Diamond Club
18 **NEW YORK,** Cat Club
20 **LONDON,** Player's Theatre
21 **PARIS,** La Locomotive
24 **MADRID,**
25 **ROME,** Piper Club
26 **MUNICH,** Parkcafe
30 **AMSTERDAM,** Paridiso Club

For these informal press conferences, David and band, minus Erdal Kizilcay performed two live numbers, picked from three songs: 'Day In, Day Out', 'Bang Bang' and '87 & Cry' and conducted an average 20 minutes of questions and answers.

The venues chosen for the conferences housed an average capacity of 300 journalists, together with groups of fans who were also allowed entry.

Concerts:

MAY
30 **ROTTERDAM,** Feyenoord Stadium
31 **ROTTERDAM,** Feyenoord Stadium

JUNE
 2 **BELGIUM,** Werchter
 6 **BERLIN,** Platz der Republik
 7 **NURBERG,** Rock AM Festival
 9 **FLORENCE,** Stadio Comunale
10 **MILAN,** Stadio San Siro
13 **HAMBURG,** Stadt Park
15 **ROME,** Stadio Flaminio
16 **ROME,** Stadio Flaminio
19 **LONDON,** Wembley Stadium
20 **LONDON,** Wembley Stadium
21 **CARDIFF,** Arms Park
23 **SUNDERLAND,** Roker Park
27 **GOTHENBURG,** Eriksberg
28 **LYON,** Gerland

JULY
 1 **VIENNA,** Praderstadium
 2 **TOULOUSE,**
 3 **PARIS,** Park de la Courneuve
 6 **MADRID,** Vincente Calderon
   Stadium
 7 **BARCELONA,** Ministadio C.F.
 8 **BARCELONA,** Ministadio C.F.
11 **DUBLIN,** Slane Castle
14 **MANCHESTER,** Maine Road
15 **MANCHESTER,** Maine Road
17 **NICE,** Stade de L'Ouest
18 **TURIN,** Stadio Communale

*The 1987 Glass Spider European tour
played a total of 27 concerts across Europe,
notably missing out Scotland, Denmark
and Norway but playing, for the first time
in Bowie's touring history, Austria, Italy,
Spain, Ireland and Wales.
All shows were outdoor venues, alternating
between stadiums and open-field concerts.*

Basic Song Set

1. Up the Hill Backwards
2. Glass Spider
3. Day In, Day Out
4. Bang, Bang
5. Absolute Beginners
6. Loving The Alien
7. China Girl
8. Fashion
9. Scary Monsters
10. All The Madmen
11. Never Let Me Down
12. Big Brother
(Drum solo for first costume change)
13. 87 & Cry
14. Heroes
15. Time Will Crawl
16. Beat Of Your Drum
17. Sons Of The Silent Age
18. New York's In Love
19. Zeroes
20. Dancing With The Big Boys
21. Let's Dance
22. Fame

Encores:
23. Time
24. Blue Jean
25. Modern Love

NB: For concerts after July 6, the following songs were added in the second section of the show and 'Zeroes' and 'New York's In Love' were omitted: 'Jean Genie', 'Young Americans', 'White Light, White Heat'. 'Time' was not performed at the following shows: Hamburg, London June 19, Cardiff, Sunderland, Manchester July 15.

Tour Personnel

Carlos Alomar – Guitar
Peter Frampton – Guitar
Erdal Kizilcay – Keyboards, Trumpet, Congas, Violin
Alan Childs – Drums
Carmine Rojas – Bass
Richard Cottle – Keyboards, Saxophone
The Dancers: **Viktor Manoei, Melissa Hurley, Spazz Attack, Stephen Nichols, Constance Marie.**
The Glass Spider Tour was directed, choreographed and staged by **David Bowie** and **Toni Basil.**

Acknowledgements:

I was fortunate enough to receive the assistance and encouragement of a great many fine folk in various countries throughout the preparation of this book – to each of whom, and those I may have inadvertently missed out, I am forever in their debt.

Gina Coyle (for sharing all the panics), Colin Prichard (my conspirator in arms!), Robin Prichard, Roeland Suurmond, Guus Hornix, Antoine Loogman, Styze Annema, Julie Stoller, Graham McDougall, Deborah and Nick McCabe at MGP, Christa Herold. Gloria Cimino, Elaine O'Dell, Peter Davis, Mandula, Katherine Solth, Keith Gale (Go and buy a bottle of wine!), Terry Fendley, Ger Peeters, Ragnhild Sorin.

My thanks to all.

For information about 'Starzone' magazine and/or any comments on this book, please write, enclosing a stamped self-addressed envelope to: David Currie, PO Box 225, Watford, Herts, WD1 7QG, England.

About the Author:

At 25, David Currie has edited and written the highly successful David Bowie magazine 'Starzone' for the past six years. Well-respected and innovative, 'Starzone' reaches a worldwide audience of Bowie followers and has become acknowledged as an authoritative voice on the life of David Bowie.

In 1985, he co-wrote and edited the book 'Starzone Interviews', also published by Omnibus Press.

In addition to his work documenting David Bowie's career, David also writes a regular rock column for a Hertfordshire newspaper and regularly writes reviews and features for other publications. He is currently writing his first fictional work, a book for children, titled 'Stories', to be published next year, as well as a biographical study of the rock group Psychedelic Furs.

David also writes and performs music and his band 'Watchmen' are staging a string of London appearances in 1988.